Seeing in the dark

Julia Dean-Richards lives in Shropshire.
Her debut novel Snailbeach Tails
was published in 2012.
This is her first book of poetry.

by the same author

Fiction
Snailbeach Tails

Poetry Blog
a place for poetry
aplaceforpoetry.wordpress.com

Julia Dean-Richards

Seeing in the dark

Fig Tree Industries

First published in 2014 by Figtree Industries,
3 Prospect Cottages, Snailbeach,
Shrewsbury SY5 0LR

1 3 5 7 9 8 6 4 2

A CIP catalogue record of this book is available from the British
Library.

This collection of poems is entirely a work of fiction.
The characters and incidents portrayed in it are a work of the
author's imagination.

ISBN 978-0-9572390-1-2

Designed and typeset in Adobe Caslon by Ray Jacobs.
Produced by Gilmour Print, www.self-publish-books.co.uk.

Papers used in this book are natural, renewable and
recyclable products sourced from well-managed forests
and certified in accordance with the rules of the Forest
Stewardship Council.

FSC
www.fsc.org
MIX
Wood from
responsible sources
FSC® C021018

for everyone

Contents

Seeing in the dark

There may be
dark moments
There may be
dark days
But look for the
magic
(Here) in so many ways

With love
Julia.

Ssshh…

On this dozing cosy cricket listening afternoon
first fire comforts soft summer bones
hot steaming apple licks our fingers
and spicy pie conversation draws close
to contemplate hibernation.

Rain

Whisky skies split splashing us to work
purposely bursting sandbagged streets
drenching pigeons grounded in the downpour
spilling the bellies of belching grids
riotous rivulets racing buses like babbling boys.
In the serious city the capillary action
of wet feet escapes us from suited restraint
and, umbrellas abandoned, arm in arm
we puddle jump.

Ladder Man

My dad was a ladder maker
constructing kit for cleaners of windows,
slow and steady in his craft, putting pride before profit,
his ladders rested upon sills and guttering
of every discerning domestic dwelling in Derbyshire.

Dad only used good unblemished wood
free from faults and knots,
he did not sell steps filled with putty mix,
berating those who operate quick and dirty fixes
which may betray the trust of unsuspecting customers.

From my dad I learned to discover deceit,
searching cracked smiles and creaking protestations,
gleaning hidden truths beneath glossed over surfaces,
his lofty craft keeping my feet firmly on the ground.

Retrospective

A lamb in a lion suit
simultaneously taller
and smaller than it seems
my youth is corruptible
but infinitely adaptable.

To those who believe in
its perfection and worth
my youth will reveal
its true identity.

Missing

L ead with an eagle's eyes
O pen canyons
S hine beacons in the dark
T H I N K W I T H M E

Star

She

burned my senses

sherbet kiss in the black-haired night

beautiful

star

More

A man flew over the corn today. I glanced him
sideways, caught his flight, an impossibility
on days when anxiety peppers experience.

He wore a long brown overcoat against the gold,
and when I did a classic double take, he had simply
done with flying and left the vicinity
of Myslow Peepers.

There is so much more in the bigger picture,
things too fast or far away to see.
But if fortune takes a shine, you may catch a glimpse
of something wonderful in the distance,
as you abseil down the abstracted slope
from Mount Busy.

Moments

We missed by one idle moment
the autumn oak leaf held aloft as faerie cup
soon dew dashed, splashed and spilled away;
a gluttonous thrush throating scores
of red rowan berries, dish of kings
one paltry clue left upon the path;
pink tongue of parched rock salt
drinking in the evening air;
a well travelled magic lantern list
and burst still burning through the leaves;
the excitement of ripe Russula mushrooms
spontaneously shattering;
but there is just time to hold one long finger
of the mother of all sunshine
as she combs the trees,
bringing burnished heaven to our hillside.

More than I bargained for!

You stood behind the counter,
my shopping in your grip;
and as you pressed hard on the till,
you spoke with narrowed lips.

"The nights are getting darker,
a chill is in the air;
we can not warm our bones at night,
what ever clothes we wear."

You squeezed my yoghurt tighter,
and looked me in the eye:
"I think evil's getting closer."
I said "Thank you and goodbye."

The Choosing

Angry as a woman ever was -
her file of life a medical lexicon
she left it all behind and plunged into the sea
assaulted by bitter rainfall on her weeping skin
body escaping from confines of wet crumpled clothes
and hair of seaweed falling through galloping waves.

All things come to an end and even pain
with all its earthly wires and strange responsibility
cannot hold us unless we will consent to stay
to keep human vigil for those who choose to swim
away.

Dark Earth

I am the underbelly -
the inside of nothing: unfixed, undefined,
not to be touched, done to, undone,
nor enough included to be cast aside.

I am after the last thought
beyond the undiscovered isle behind dying eyes,
beneath a broken tongue which may not speak,
in the well of deep behind angry teeth.

I am postliminary in-consequence
dangling over the lip of impossible.

Yet still, I am!

Pocket

If I should ever have to choose to be
a pocket or a coat, my answer is a pocket, plain.
Oh yes, to wrap the world in warm is fine,
to comfort children caught by snow or storm,
to zip and tuck unhappy souls on luckless roads,
no doubt. But still I think I wouldn't choose to be
a winter coat.

Why then, you ask, a pocket?

If I may catch the crumbs of something good and
gone, contain the angry fist, relax the anxious palm;
if I may hold a handkerchief where precious tears are
pressed, keep safe a favourite glove,
or perhaps a letter felt and left;
if I may hold a secret till it's ready to be spoke,
then a pocket plain and simple would I choose
above a coat.

Big Foot

It paid no respect, would
not do as we said, just
kept jumping around, as if
beans worked its head. It
was only a toy, but
it thought it was real, and
was acting as though it
could think, grow and feel. We
didn't quite know what
its next move would be if
we told it to go, so
we asked it for tea. Now it
sits down for meals, though
we know it can't eat, but
I guess we're quite fond of
the thing with big feet.

Winter Chill

The grandfather clock coughs
and then they are all at it,
armchairs belch their stuffing,
tables drop all their leaves, cushions deflate.

The radiator complains of a temperature;
the bed winces when I lie on it, so
I perch near the moaning fish tank
watching eczema paint peel from sore throat walls.

Later, I grab my guitar, but it winges and slides
out of tune with the day,
offending the aching ears of the television
which begs me to turn the sound down
real low.

Offering

In the old place,
as you snatched your gaze away from me,
I saw our futures in the furniture behind your head,
carved from antithesis, set in stone;
you rolled your eyes across an over - stretched
conversation, and years flexed and flew.

While I pirouetted into semi dark,
you stuck your colours to the nearest domestic lamp
and remained stoically moth-like.
I hardly dare knock at our last closed door,
fearing the beat of distressed wings,
but I come with fresh baked anodyne,
and if you answer,
it will make this new morning blossom.

Gone

Soon you will be to me
absent as moon trees
distant as a lonely prayer on ancient lips
intangible as a strong forgotten taste.

Like an improbable hypothesis
snatched from the breath of a wayward student
you will wing it into the theoretical landscape
shape shifting then
less now than nothing
leaving only dust motes and regret
to mark your passing.

Transition

The train is leaving, but there is the head of a child
Resolutely wedged in my door of change
A sense of submerging as the old breath runs out
Nasty phobias manifest at times like this
Surrendering, the final click elicits a sick shiver.

I begin again with an awkward moment.

This is how life pans out on my emergence
I walk strangely into a squeaky new room
Only when I am firmly ensconced, do I open my eyes.

Now though, once again, my mind is in the gap.

Mind the gap! Mind the gap!

Sunday

Cards, did you ever stand?
Or was my brilliant house of hearts,
young fumbling fingers darting in
to rebuild broken parts,
a childish and imagined thing
dreamed up by chilly rooms?
Do you recall the way we played
on Sunday afternoons?

In our separate world were marbles,
and a box of dominoes,
each indent to be thumbed,
the numbers nought to six in rows,
each globe a tiny planet trapped,
in subtle colour rolled,
all added up when I was very young
and they were old.

And when they called me in at last,
I boxed and bagged my friends,
to leave disgruntled kings and queens
and keepsies in the end.
One hand still cupped around a shell
in which I hear the sea,
I peer through dust of lemon cake
washed down with grown-up tea.

The Curator

Economically, it was a difficult time,
women itched in woollen scarves,
men stamped their frosted minds,
a cruel wind blew till their steaming chips were down.

Socially, it was a treacherous climb:
he clung to the frozen earth with hooked toes

v
e
r
t
i
c
a
l
l
y

impossible, pebbles snapping like dragons' teeth,
stressed grass grazing his aching knees.

Astrologically, he read the perfect sign
and chose this day to set his sight
at the hill above vast unmolested sea.

At the summit
he would put down his heavy pack,
lean his broad back against a small patch of
undamaged sky and watch history unfold.

Moon Man

There is a man sits in our crescent moon tonight
with jocular face and monocle.
Hunter-warriors beware,
he will rock away this precious slice of light
should you prey on easy meat
from a high-handed horse.

There is a man sits in our crescent moon tonight
tickling xylophones with whiskery fingers.
As ice drops flicker
give time over haste to winter tunes,
to taste his gruffle-sung stories
of stars and wonderment.

There is a man sits in our crescent moon tonight
making immortal space for us.
He cradles kindness in extraordinarily long arms,
and gifts weary travellers with chuckling beneficence.

Computer Generation

He was once a real boy;
distinctly she remembers him
holding her hand and looking her in the eye.

These days, to gain his attention
she wears prescription 3D glasses
and sits in a life-simulating gaming chair;
unsure whether the blurred edges he exhibits
are the result of his stereoscopic obsession,
a definite change in generational perspective,
or the tears in her empty nest eyes.

Old Year

Old Year rolls towards the edge:
all but cliff-tipped and crown-cropped,
he grizzles over sticky mince pies
and thrice cooked turkey,
downs a last guzzle of mulled liquor
and stuffs his pockets with fruit cake.

He will have none of party preparation -
"like celebrating my own execution".
Instead, he catches up on old TV,
plays Cluedo with the kids, who call him Mr Black,
and packs for emergencies:
no-one knows how it will happen this time.

Still, warm gloves, tin of family biscuits,
and swimming goggles,
he's ready to put both his legs in one elastic
and catapult himself into the next place.
If it turns out less than nice,
chances are, he won't be there for long:
Years generally quit before outstaying their welcome.

Fire

Marking our winters together,
first up in the morning checks the embers,
so any vital signs might be rekindled.

Failing that, I journey out to fetch the coal,
perhaps a well seasoned cherry log, our treat,
odour – vermillion. Slipper shod round to the shed,
contemplating cold patterned leavings in the snow.

I consider the teeth clenched path;
you warm in tangled bed,
then, lamenting the lazy left last time bucket,
slide down to empty tinker crunch ash,
playing the ice orchestra
and wishing above all for wellies.

Darling, the clinker hill reaches the sky,
in far off spring we will push it down
to the ditch below the snow line,
between where we live and the cows.

Swinging up to the house to scrunch last week's news,
I lay morning sticks crackling
from an orange string bag,
then, sparingly, the coal, but leave room for breath.
Striking a match I turn on the life support,
a tender touch paper, sharing the conviction that
our winter child will thrive.

Rainbow

Today, in the town squares of all great cities
around this beautiful globe,
we will, by common consent, remove divisive flags
hung by history's tainted shreds of angry pride;
folding them away like old aunty's table cloths.

And see draped instead, from mountain heights,
a more fantastic sight: our real heritage.
Reflective of all earth's passion and intensity
absorbing in amazement all our pain,
this is our rainbow - and the music of a shared song.

Aunty

This morning in your honour I boiled an egg
a simple act to cut through time
eating comfort with a small spoon.
It brought back the red glow of your hearth
re-instated the sound of knitting needles
and made true again the knowledge that here was
a safe place for as long as I chose to stay.

The Inside

I have done a lot of thinking
about the inside of things.

Today I built a dome
one foot square
and solid snow.

Inside were the animals
I would have made
if the snow didn't
get stuck on my gloves
and crumble in my hands.
A moose
and a mole.

The moose had long, strong legs
and an intelligent, wet nose.
He put his head down
into the snow
and nuzzled

until he found a piece of green,
then chewed thoughtfully
whilst contemplating the upstairs window.
He seemed surprised
that humans
have such long legs
they need windows that high up.

The mole poked his snowy bonce
out of the tired ground
and peered with blind eyes
upon the bright sky.
I think he was glad
I would have made him.

I have done a lot of thinking
about the inside of things.

Sleepers

We are brickless, backless turtles
ridden by nightmares;
nemesis of ideals, monstrous victims of blind eyes,
walked upon inadvertently by vulnerable feet.

Keen-edged conceit is a knife that steals amongst us,
slashing our flimsy shelters with its silver tongue,
so we must run out shivering in the rain.

Dawn Again

Our Birth Day breaks,
pouring sand through quickened senses,
restoring shine to tarnished self-belief.
Wrapped in miracles we become anew
beautiful in a small animal way,
and stride with eyes lifted in purpose,
opposing damaged feet.

Seeing in the Dark

They tipped me from a hefty perambulator
into a wooden pen, until I was measured up
for a red metal horse with fixed wheels,
graduating to a blue and yellow bike.

Hurtling between stabilisers, curiosity took
my senses, and the wrong kind of accelerator
drove me into black tyre valley,
where the predominant smell is petrol
caught in dirty underclothes.

Old enough to break the law
my new mode was tax free, hot-wired,
with a rabbit in the back seat:
fun cars with sad endings.

I codged together a monocycle
made from disapproving eyes,
and rode naked, at breakneck speed,
to the next junction. Parked.

On the road again, it pays to keep
a bed on your back and
loose change in your ashtray.
It pays to check your fuses, keep your head
and turn your lights on.
That way you have a chance of seeing in the dark.

Hand Recital

These two hands
are both my boundaries and my open gate
raised up to signify life and catch my breath,
and as I ponder they take the pen to write,
dipping sotto voce ink, and hearing hidden passion
with sentient finger tips.

How these two friends
push and press and work together,
folding over dough in pas des deux parenthesis,
gathering to cup a warming brew
or comb through hair,
iced blue in deep snow pockets,
in summer – full red and ripe.

Comfortable in prayer,
who would judge these anguished two
for uncommon deviation;
a desperate grab in tightened times?

Or ignited in knuckled protest,
closing angry fists as if to fight?
Look down then to your left and to your right.

My industrious two return to sew and knit and thread
and wrap and cut and spread and meet and reassure
and weave between expression and caress.
And when you go they'll wave and wipe,
go mix a cake.

Each day they pick and pour and weigh,
these two hands.
In doubt they shift and shy,
but regrouping bear me up, my loyal retainers,
remaining after fair has faded,
brushing ebb and flow as time is plucked and dropped.

In Memory

My memory is
a tailored suit black cuff button
rolled flipped and wedged between dusty wainscot
and wooden floor.

It is four heavy old pennies balanced and stacked
beneath the leg of a lopsided make-do desk.

And then I may take the middle
of a punched paper hole
scuffed and left by the soul of a Brogue.

In perpetuity it will bear faintest traces
of the stale scent of slim cigars
emanating from a plastic-lined basket-work bin.

It will not be wiped either
by its one string slither of a shedding mop.

There will be a sound too -
a sound insistent as a stylophone;
like the thrum of Anglia cars through thin windows.

And oh yes, its colours will always be orange -
orange and bottle green.

Family Ties

We meet to consider old stitches;
knotted to the past by red thread,
which, dangling still between us,
is tensioned by remembrance.

Our fragile family quilt,
sewn haphazardly by unpractised hands,
requires the nimble unpick of constituent parts
and the renewal of worn twine.

Too long we sensitive seamsters
put aside the intricacies of a trying task,
when the damaged beauty of our creased cloth
can be redressed with candor, and restored.

Bear

In the high street you turn from Ursula,
that small wreaking bear in a fine old coat:
well worn dichlorobenzenated reminder
of an otherwise wasted life.

Up and down she pads, from dawn to dark,
claws clicking past embarrassed charity,
rather proffering that magnificent maned neck
to the limp lasso of wet and greedy punters.

Her hunted life is heft and loaded into BMWs,
to be stuffed and tipped back later, sore and sober,
that fabulous bear coat torn and taken from her,
the remains of its wilderness scratching at her back.

The Spirit of Accord

Conjoined by circumstance, we were as twins,
collective fate upon respective dials;
you docked your pirate ship inside my lines
and blocked me with uncompromising sails.

To square the round we drew our swords to fight,
inflicting wrath on anchored minds with spears;
decisions ground with sharp wit edged with spite,
in altercation boxed the other's ears.

In case you tried to sail I slung my stones,
and what I strove to build you ran to spoil;
you flared your nostrils, stamped upon my bones,
I danced on pins to pitch my burning oil.

You curdled coffee with your sour grapes,
my rancid comments rattled down our time;
but now you're gone I miss our fierce debates,
it seems as though your voice was also mine.

Lily

From this stricken bridge, our pickled Lily
is a ragged and a snarling twig
stuck fast between grey stones.
Whilst all around
cross Eddies feud and weave,
she brooks her gall, suspended.

Who knows, should snagged forgiveness
truly rip and run again,
the river, reprieved, may turn to smile,
and Lily's spoiled white lips
would twist and split: a pretty boat.

Her veil, pulled low to save that petalled face,
could raise into a hopeful sail
and pistilled spirit bend and dip
to fast row Lily, blemished but aglow,
to steep her days without bondage and regret
in turbulent regatta.

Breakfast Hymn

Walk out with me in morning feet,
along the edge of spring,
still steeped in snow, our woollen coats
pulled hard against the wind.
There, gowned and slippered, see she stands,
Nature is summoning the land:

It's time to shine
It's time to shine
She holds the sunlight in her hand.

Walk out with me in morning feet,
and catch the swooshing loud,
of Nature smoothing cotton sheets
and plumping pillow clouds.
She lifts the verdant grass to grow
and lusty, showered in the dew,

It's time to shine
It's time to shine
will dress our hillside all anew.

Walk out with me in morning feet,
to greet the waking day,
when preparations are complete
and humans on their way.
Our breakfast on the quilted hill
a secret unrevealed, until

It's time to shine
It's time to shine
She sweeps our breadcrumbs from her sill.